Ozana Giusca

Business Unlimited
Smarter Profits Faster

- Volume 4 -

Get the Most out of Your Team

101
Zero-Cost
Tactics to Take
Your Company
to the Next
Level

Amaze Yourself With What YOU Can Achieve Further!

Copyright © 2017 Ozana Giusca
All rights reserved.

ISBN-13: 978-1978361874
ISBN-10: 1978361874

To all the business owners and entrepreneurs I have worked with: thank you for entrusting me with growing your business.

To my team, who have put so much effort into building Tooliers, the high-end business growth tools and programs that are transforming businesses around the world, a big thank you for going through the ups and downs with me.

Thank you for helping me with this book. We wouldn't be here without your dedication and contribution!

I would like to name the Tooliers core team: Vali, Dragos, Sorana & Catalina. You are like family to me! I am so grateful you joined me in my journey!

Table of Contents

Foreword	V
Preface	VII
My Story	IX
Introduction	1
Bonus • Steady Growth - Systematize Your Business	4
Tactic #1 • Follow a System	5
Note: Tactics #2 - #44 are in Volumes 1-3	
Get the Most out of Your Team	12
Tactic #45 • Maximize Your Team's Commitment	13
Tactic #46 • Attract the Right Mix	17
Tactic #47 • Retain Those Employees Who Fit In	21
Tactic #48 • Make Sure that Your Employees Know What the Company Expects of Them	24
Tactic #49 • Ensure Your Employees Know Your Company's Purpose	28
Tactic #50 • Implement a Massive Action Plan	32
Tactic #51 • Share Short-Term and Medium-Term Goals with Everyone in the Company	36
Tactic #52 • Set S-M-A-R-T Objectives…	40
Tactic #53 • Train Your Sales Staff Exceptionally Well	44
Tactic #54 • Regularly Monitor the Motivation of Your Staff	47
Tactic #55 • Align the Individual Goals of Your Staff with Company Goals	52
Tactic #56 • Don't Use Money to Motivate Your Staff	56
Smart Business System™	60
Bonus • Love Letter	72
Love Letter Template	74
Love Letter Example	75
Glossary of Terms	78

Foreword

The world is changing so fast. These events are opportunities for those who grab them, and at the same time can negatively affect those who do not take action. Most small businesses find it harder to break through their current level. They reach a plateau and do not know what step to take next, or go beyond 'small' and lose the plot.

There is so much information available now about how to run a successful business, but the challenge is to find meaning within this information and to use it appropriately to optimize and grow your business. In my experience as a small business consultant, I have seen a lot of business owners who cannot simply and quickly explain what they do, let alone generate interest and sell their products or services. I also see that entrepreneurs have dreams and goals, yet 80% of their time is spent on things that have no link whatsoever with their objectives. If they do not focus on what is needed to achieve their goals, how can they get there?

If you are looking for a very hands-on approach to building your business from the ground up, Ozana has nailed it in *Business Unlimited.* What a purposeful read for anyone who is an entrepreneur or small business owner. As you continue on your business or career journey, you will face real challenges that may deter you from achieving your biggest goals. The tactics in this book will keep you on track and help you reach your goals in record time.

In our lives we have the opportunity to do it the hard way or to learn from what the experts do, and then do it better. Ozana has been trained by some of the best in the business, including business and marketing guru Jay Abraham. In this new book you will discover key observations and ingredients to create even more success in your life and business. The real-world examples, as well as the practical exercises at the end of each tactic, also ensure this is a user-friendly manual to reaching business success.

Foreword

In *Business Unlimited*, you will learn to see the bigger picture of your business as well as discover the importance of *systematically* improving it; that is, by prioritizing and focusing on those areas that most need improvement. You will learn to identify your best customers; let go of any customers who do not lift your business; learn from your competitors; and fulfil the core purpose of every business: providing *real value* to your customers. You will also discover how creating the right kind of partnerships will grow your business with little extra effort on your part. Business owners will find the tactics on closing sales and creating urgency especially valuable. You will also see how essential it is to build relationships both with your best customers and your team.

This book is also brutally honest about areas in which business owners tend to waste time and resources – and provides a wealth of best practices for time management; this includes a reminder to employ the time-saving advantages of certain technologies. You will also be encouraged to reflect and act upon your role as a leader and to go beyond merely managing your business to making sure it leads to the kind of life and lifestyle you desire. Aspects like personal branding, networking and being open to change are also discussed. Finally, you will clarify your vision in order to take your brand into the future and be left with a business that is dynamic and that constantly strives for – and achieves – improvement and growth.

The bottom line: if you are ready to increase your success rate today, take the time to read this mind-expanding book two to three times, and then implement the ideas that are shared here.

Bill Walsh

America's Small Business Expert

Website: billwalsh360.com

Preface

If you answer YES! to any of these statements, this book is for you.

- You have achieved some success with your business, but seem unable to grow it further.
- You are not satisfied with where your business is.
- You are not getting enough from your business (you are not getting enough recognition or enough money, or you have not succeeded in fully achieving your Objectives).
- Work is taking over your life and you have no time for family, relaxation, or travel.
- You are still struggling to make a living.
- You are bored with your work! You want something more challenging and fun.
- You are missing something, but you're not sure exactly what.
- There are some areas you do not understand (for example, finance) or you are passionate about your product, but you cannot sell it.
- You just want to be sure that you are on top of things and that your business is on the right track.
- You have some ideas for new businesses, but are not quite sure how to go about it.
- You want new challenges, but you need your current business to continue to run for various reasons (financial, community).
- Your turnover and/or profits have started decreasing.
- You can anticipate a disaster but you cannot tell what exactly is happening.
- Your best employees have started to leave.
- You have lost your biggest client.
- You seem to deliver good quality but your clients are still not prepared to pay what you'd like for your products.
- There has been a recent change in your company's industry or outside

environment and this has had a great impact on your business.
- You and your staff are working too hard and it is just not fair on any of you (especially given the results you achieve).
- You consider your company a victim of your crisis, a system, or something else.
- Your business has stopped serving the community.
- Your business is growing quickly and you are struggling to manage it. It is becoming too complex for you to run on your own.
- Your life is too stressful. There are just too many problems that need to be solved by you, the business owner.
- You and your co-owners have trouble running the business together.
- Your business has started experiencing problems or you foresee problems, but you don't know what to do about them.
- You have accumulated too much debt in your company and can no longer sustain it.
- You simply want to discover the latest strategies that Fortune 500 companies use for their success!

My Story

I want to take a few minutes to ask you the questions that are on every small business owner's mind:

- What is the REAL secret behind businesses that generate more profits while their owners are enjoying life and doing what they want, when they want?
- Can I get more customers to call us instead of *us* chasing *them*?
- How can I get a great team of committed employees to work hard so we grow the business together?
- Is there any way to feel happier with my business and really achieve what I set my mind to?
- Ultimately, how can I, a small business owner, entrepreneur or freelance expert, make a difference in the world?

I get asked these questions all the time and it's why I wrote this book. Via this book, the tools, programs, events we deliver, I provide the answers to these questions, and many more.

Before you dig in, let me tell you a little about myself…

In 2007 my life seemed perfect. I was a rising star, doing everything most people would love to do.

After attaining my MBA from Cass Business School, London in 2000, I worked in the City for a few years. In 2003, I set up my own consulting firm, where I advised on selling a few companies and raised hundreds of millions in bank finance for various projects.

While my business generated a decent income, I knew I was on my way to support other entrepreneurs help more people and make a bigger impact.

With a team of 12 consultants, I was living my dream. I could party, travel, wear my favorite brands…

My Story

I bought a flat, then another one, then an office for our company, a new car... until the financial crisis hit my business badly, as happened with thousands of businesses around the world.

All of a sudden money stopped flowing in. The banks withdrew from financing our transactions; those hundreds of thousands of dollars in success fees never arrived; and ongoing consulting projects got put on hold. No more new business meant no more cash.

Imagine: By January 2009, I had let most of my team go. For me, they were not just staff, they were *family*. And they were damn good at what they did.

With more than a million dollars in debt, I could no longer pay the bank. Many sleepless nights followed... I felt ashamed, convinced people would point a finger at me, accuse me of not paying my debts. I got scared thinking about a potential bad credit rating and that I might never be able to get a loan again.

I felt my reputation as an honest, trustworthy businessperson was ruined as I couldn't pay my debts.

I had no money coming in and was borrowing on a monthly basis to pay my two remaining staff members. I was driving to my father every weekend to get food for the week for me and my partner.

It seemed that every phone call I got, every email I received, brought more bad news.

Watch this: my phone service provider threatening to end my contract should I not pay my bills. Imagine trying to save a business without a phone connection or access to the internet!

That was it, I decided. *Enough!* I borrowed more money and paid for an event in London where 15 successful entrepreneurs shared their strategies on how they became profitable. I learned about online marketing, selling one-to-many via events and social media advertising. Most importantly I realized the need to be visible to the right audience.

x

How many of these tactics do you think I applied? None! Because I soon realized I was in the wrong business anyway. Yep, this was my biggest take-away from the conference. I realized there was nothing special about me or my business, nothing that would get clients to choose our services.

There were too many people doing the same thing, making it difficult to differentiate myself.

As I had all this cutting edge knowledge, I started applying it to the businesses of former clients, and friends. And *this* is how I started earning again...

It turned out my consulting business was not the only business lacking proper business knowledge! In fact, most small businesses lack such knowledge – they are usually set up based on an opportunity the founder sees, based on the founder's skills and abilities. Yet businesses are complex and no entrepreneur can know it all; certainly no one can handle everything.

I also discovered my special gift: being able to identify where a business is leaving money on the table and how they can double or even triple their profits by making a few important changes.

My skill became immediately obvious as I managed to achieve:

- **30% increase in Sales within a month** for a client in hospitality (hotel) and a **287% increase in their online bookings within three months.** Their occupancy rate was 10% when we started working together – now it's in excess of 50%.

- **8 Sales during the first workshop** for a weight loss solution – a full house event achieved within five days of promotion. In fact, we had to close the doors and leave people outside disappointed.

- **$40,000 in Sales generated for a book** that had been sitting idle on Amazon before

With the right tools YOU too can turn your business around

My Story

we started working with the author/chiropractor.

- **15% increase in Sales** for the main distributor of promotional materials, who already had 50% market share.

Over the past three years, I have personally helped more than 100 companies achieve massive growth. Some companies increased Sales by 30% within the first month of working with us; others tripled their Sales within a year.

I put all the knowledge I gathered – and much more – into what is today known as **Business Lens™**, a toolkit to identify what business owners don't do well or enough of in their company. This is **a tool that reveals the naked truth about any business**. It measures, mathematically, the gap between your company and Best Practices. The bigger the gap, the more growth potential the company has. Plus, it shows business owners where they need to focus to maximize Sales and profits.

This was the start of Tooliers, the platform with Smart Business solutions for small enterprises to increase profitability and become leaders in their niche. We now have clients around the globe and what's most important is not that we are making money, but that we help those who need us and our tools to smarten their businesses and achieve bigger profits faster.

Above all, I am proud of having built something that lasts beyond me. I know people will benefit from my current activities even after I am no longer here.

What's really in it for me? Or you?

> *When you focus on the right things in your business, you have the recipe to success*

My Story

FREEDOM!

The freedom to do what I want, when I want; to live anywhere in the world... and most importantly to be ME!

> *So what does this have to do with you and your business?*

You too can have the FREEDOM you want!

And I guess this is one reason you are reading this – you know you can do more and you want to.

The economy changes rapidly these days. As a small business owner, it is easy to run your business as if lost in a dark forest, thinking only of *survival*. You might forget about the destination. You are most likely involved with paying the next bill, dealing with a crisis after your best employee has left, trying to make up for that lost customer, deciding what kind of paper to buy for the copy machine and many other activities that keep you 'busy' and working hard.

But do you work *smart*? What if there was **a better way to achieve those dreams** you had when you started your business?

One third of business owners **want to grow their businesses, but don't know how and where to start**. The rest would like to maintain their business. The reality, however, is that 80% of businesses fail in the first five years and 96% in the first 10 years (this according to Michael Gerber, author of The *E-Myth*).

These facts also inspired me to write this book. I want to help YOU, a business owner, to *enjoy* your entrepreneurship. I want to help driven entrepreneurs just like you to achieve the success you deserve.

Business Unlimited is a collection of Best Practices I have seen and learned during my 20-year career in professional services. I learned about these tactics from seminars, workshops, conferences and summits,

My Story

and I have tried and tested them on my business and on our clients' businesses. When you master the tactics that follow, you will be able to compete with multinational companies, with Fortune 500 companies, as their equal. Because you know what? They use exactly the same tactics you are about to discover.

This book is part of my mission to empower 1,000,000 entrepreneurs to change the world while they achieve their personal and professional objectives fast, with ease.

Happy reading and enjoy the transformation of your business!

Ozana

Your Smarter Profits Accelerator

P.S. If you are serious about growing your Sales and profits, raising your profile and helping way more people, I invite you to join any of my online or live Master Classes and bootcamps.

Visit My Events Page *(www.ozanagiusca.com/my-events)* to get the updated schedule of my events and register to those most suitable for you.

Why have I written this book?

I wrote this book because I believe YOU can achieve much more especially in today's economy, which is the best possible environment for driven entrepreneurs and small businesses to really take off and finally get to the next level, especially because of the Internet and technology developments.

I believe that small businesses are changing the world and making it a better place... provided they deploy the right systems. Thus, this book is about a systematic approach to business so you achieve your dreams and gain the respect you deserve.

Turning around my own company from the brink of bankruptcy in 2008 to a business selling on all continents was an incredible journey. Having been through 3 years with no sales (before Tooliers took off), I made every possible mistake. I also realised that business can be fun. So I made it my mission to empower 1,000,000 entrepreneurs to make a bigger impact, by proving them with full clarity on their business, and, of course, the right tools. Bottom line, I want to reduce the entrepreneurial struggle by encouraging small business owners and experts to first think strategically and then implement any tactic they consider. This way, they finally get results quickly with no stress or overwhelm.

This book is about sharing some of the lessons we've learnt so you build a profitable business and unleash your unlimited potential... **hence BUSINESS UNLIMITED**.

You hear me talk about Smart Business, which is the vehicle to get there... A Smart Business is flexible in approach, leverages what you have and know, and systematically attracts clients online so you scale and grow exponentially. This, of course, enables you, its founder and commander, to be anywhere you want, and not chained to your desk 16 hours per day.

My Story

Regardless of being early stage or a successful entrepreneur, if you are driven to achieve more, to create more value, to serve more people and improve their lives while you get what you want, then I would love to support you in your journey.

Let's change the world together!

Introduction

How to use this book

You don't have to start with Tactic 1, or to read this collection chronologically. Start with the tactic that feels the most interesting to you. Each tactic addresses a different Stage of a business. You may find one tactic more relevant than another. Read the relevant ones first and feel free to jump from one tactic to another.

You will see that each of the 101 Tactics concludes with a short exercise that will make it easy to apply the tactic to your business. If you are serious about growing your business, it is essential that you *decide how to apply* the tactic you have just read and *do the exercises* that follow. While doing the exercises, write down whatever comes to mind.

Don't get overwhelmed by all the information in this book. You don't have to use it all at once. However, you will be surprised by how much of this book applies to you and your business. Take the knowledge on board, and don't get desperate if you can't find a way of using it on the spot. The more you practice using these tactics, the more ideas you will get – in time you may even find ways to use those tactics you thought were not relevant to your business.

Revisit the book as your business Needs and Goals change. Reread certain tactics, or tackle new ones. This book may well become your 'Bible for a Smarter Business'.

Introduction

The finer details

Definitions of all words or terms that appear in **bold and italics** or starting with Caps can be found in the Glossary of Terms.

I use **customer** as a generic term. In your industry, you may prefer the word client, visitor, guest, user, or patient, for example.

I use examples from **a range of industries**. Feel free to adapt and apply the tactics to your own business.

Throughout the book, I use **products** and **services** interchangeably. Note, however, that an **offering** is not the same as a product or service. For our purposes, an offering refers to the product or service combined with its price, packaging and positioning. So, product X as offering A is sold for $100 as a stand-alone product. Product X could also be packaged as offering B, which includes another item or addresses a different market or just has a different packaging, and sells for $200.

Example:

> *Cashew nuts can be sold in large quantities (tons) to wholesalers, who then repackage the nuts in smaller quantities (say 1 kilogram) to be sold at the market. Those same cashew nuts can be sold in supermarkets in packs of 300 grams; these look more attractive and command a higher price. Or the cashew nuts can be sold per 100 grams in a high-end bar, for a premium price.*
>
> *The product is the same – cashew nuts – but with different packaging and/or positioning, it becomes a different offering and commands a different price.*
>
> *The target market could be the same or different. I could be buying a 1 kg pack at the market, but I could also buy the 300 gram packs in gas stations.*

Introducing Tooliers®

Tooliers® (www.tooliers.com) is THE latform with high-end business growth solutions to empower entrepreneurs to build their SMART business so they increase profitability, reduce struggle and become leaders in their niche.

Business Lens™ is the digital mirror of your business. It shows you the naked truth about your business. It shows your unrealized growth potential.

Business Lens™ Diagnosis is the process of using Business Lens™ to perform a full analysis of your business, which identifies the areas that need more of your attention so you take your business to the next level.

Business Doctor is one of our growth programs, where we perform the Business Lens™ Diagnosis, and issue suggestions and recommendations for tactics and strategies to execute, so you grow your business immediately as well as long term.

Businesses don't grow unless people grow. You rock! By reading this book, you are enabling personal growth together with business growth!

Bonus:
Steady Growth -
Systematize Your Business

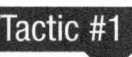

Follow a System

> *Focus your efforts exactly where they are required as your business grows*

I have created the **Business Growth Focus Formula** (see below) because so often I see business owners focusing on the wrong things. You want to do what you like to do, or what you are best at and this is fine to a certain extent. But if you want to have a *highly successful business*, you need to approach it systematically, and change Focus according to which Stage your business is at. Focus doesn't mean you only work on a certain area of your business or that you do it all by yourself. It means you **concentrate your efforts on a particular area of your business at a particular time.** It also means that you learn more about that area. Of course, you can involve Experts and you can Delegate, as long as this area is where your mind is. Even if you outsource, you inevitably acquire more knowledge in that area.

> *Be disciplined and Focus on what you have to in order to reach your Objectives and fulfill your dreams*

The idea is simple: your Focus, as the owner of the business, moves from 'Sales' to 'Sources and Resources' to 'Systems', as your company grows. This is the **best business growth strategy**. Focusing on one part of the business does not mean that you *only* deal with that part. It means, say, that you allocate half of your time to it, while the other half is split between anything else you would normally deal with. Above all, you, as the business owner, must focus on what needs your Focus, even if it is not necessarily what you *like* doing.

Let's talk about each area of a business:

Business Growth Focus Formula

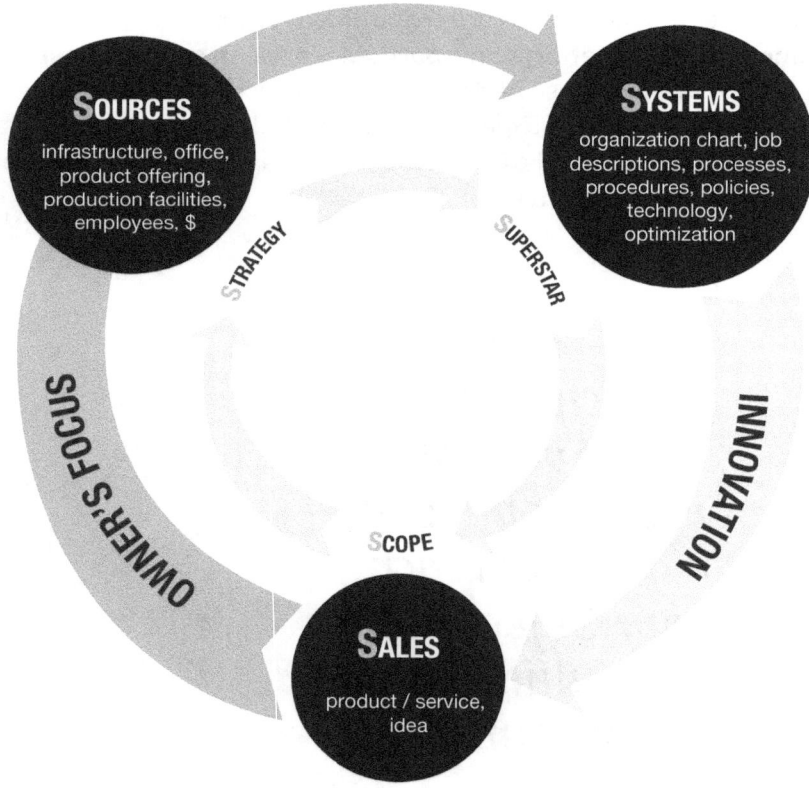

1 Focus on Sales

When you are at the beginning with your business, or when you launch a new product or open a new location. 'Sales' is split into two parts:

(i) selling your product or service;

(ii) selling your idea.

Selling your product or service is what you would generally understand as: giving your product / service to your customer in exchange for money (the price paid).

Selling your idea means getting people to buy into what you are doing. To share your dream, your vision and to get others excited about it. Selling your idea to current employees, potential employees, partners, suppliers, banks and any other person who is necessary to run the business smoothly, is as important as selling your product. You cannot create a business on your own. To achieve your Objectives, you need people around you. And those people don't join just because you think they should. It is tempting to believe they see and understand as you do, but they don't. You have to give them reasons to opt in, just as you give reasons to your customers to buy your product.

During this Stage, you have only a **Scope**. You know where you want to get to, but it is still flexible. You need the market reaction and partners' Feedback in order to ensure you have the right product, the right offering, both for your *customers* and for your business partners. The offering for the *customer* is a widely used concept: 'Buy this product for this price because it solves this problem in this way.' The offer for *business partners* sounds something like this: 'Bring customers to our business and you get x% from all the money they spend with us.' This is how you have to think of the Value proposition for your customers and your business partners. All parties have to win. And everything has to make sense and be clear from the outset.

2 Focus on Sources and Resources

Once your product or service sells by itself; in other words, when customers buy your product or service without you having to convince each of them individually. By 'Sources' I mean everything that enables you to deliver to your customer; that is, your overall infrastructure: production facility, office space, logistics, as well as your employees and money to buy raw materials and invest in further growth. No point selling if you can't deliver, right?

When you have gotten to this phase, **you have a Strategy in place.** Now that you know what and how you sell, and for how much, you can create Specific Objectives and a clear path to achieving them.

3 Focus on System

When you are confident that you have a product that sells and that you can deliver and satisfy your customer. By 'Systems', I mean organizational charts, job descriptions, processes, procedures, policies, IT system, and potentially CRM / ERP (software to help with planning and managing your Resources and your customers).

In this phase you **consolidate what you have**; you organize things internally and clean up your mess. By this Stage, you and your staff have tried various ways of producing and delivering Value and you now know who does what in your company, and how. It is therefore time to document everything that is happening in your company, to put order in place. This helps you and your current employees to better understand how things are being done in your company and to become more efficient. Having these Systems in place also makes for an easier and more efficient process when you bring new people into your organization. You have 'machinery' that works, effectively and efficiently.

What you care about now is **becoming a Superstar Company**. By 'Superstar', I mean being the best in your niche. If you think of your industry as a pyramid, there is only one company on top, a few on the second layer, then the third, and so on... until the bottom, where you find plenty of companies. Your Objective is to **get as close as possible to the top**. Why? Because if anything destructive happens in the economy or in your industry, or if anything happens that can adversely affect your business, you hardly feel it if you are on top. The financial crisis in 2008 resulted in many companies going bankrupt or being close to bankrupt – this is because they were at the bottom of the pyramid in their niche. If a tsunami comes, or the state does construction on the road in front of your shop or office, you need to be in such a strong position that your business does not suffer. This is being a Superstar Company.

After Systems are in place, you need to focus on **Innovation** if you want to take your company to the next level, in which case you go back to Sales in another growth cycle. Alternatively, you retire or sell your company (or you leave it as is and continue to manage 'in the business', which may eventually go downhill).

> *Shift Focus as your company develops and grows*

TAKE ACTION NOW!

Based on the Stage of your business development, decide which of the three areas discussed above requires your Focus. Write it down:

_____
_____
_____
_____
_____
_____

What are your biggest current Challenges? Write these here; then use the tactics in this book to find ways of overcoming these Challenges.

Challenge 1:
_____
_____

Challenge 2:
_____
_____

Challenge 3:
_____
_____

Challenge 4:
_____
_____

Challenge 5:
_____
_____

Get the Most out of Your Team

 Tactic #45

Get the Most out of Your Team

Maximize Your Team's Commitment

Care for your employees

Keeping your staff committed should be one of your Priorities. When people are committed they will put in the time, effort and energy to achieve the results expected of them. When they are not committed they will do the minimum possible, waiting for the time to pass before they get their paycheck.

Employee Engagement is a key factor for your business's success and directly impacts productivity and employee retention. But what is Employee Engagement? I think of it as a meaningful two-way relationship: commitment from the employee to the company and care by the company for employee. A 2012 Gallup study suggests that only 30% of U.S. employees are engaged at work, and barely 13% of employees worldwide are engaged. Yet a happy employee delivers better results and for a longer period of time.

The tricky part is that the recipe for happiness differs from one person to another. As the owner / leader it is your responsibility to consider each individual's particularities. **Don't for a moment think that everyone is Motivated by money.** If they were, they would have set up their own company (or become mercenaries!). Today's employees expect a partnership with their employer / company. They can't be treated merely as bodies or numbers (even if this is how you think of them privately).

People who get plus / minus 10% of the average salary for their level are happy with their pay.

Most people who leave their job leave because they are not happy with the working environment. 86% of sales people who leave, leave because of a bad relationship with their superior.

You might have allocated a budget to your managers to take their teams for lunch once a month – and this is more than any other company in your industry does. You may be right, but do you have any idea what they talk about during that lunch? Do they all bitch and moan about their job or do they talk about movies? Or does the manager take their time to understand what Motivates the team members, what they expect from the company, what their dreams are, and who they really are?

Take a step back and reflect on how Motivated the managers in your company are... how 'engaged' they are with your business. You are unlikely to have highly Motivated people in your company if their managers are not Motivated. Ensure that all key influencers in your business walk their talk and set a good example of commitment to the rest of the staff.

> *Managers influence your team.*
> *Ensure they are a good example!*

Make it work for you!

Imagine a team in which direct supervisors observe members in action, ask for Feedback, identify the root causes of employee concerns, and then follow through with meaningful improvements. Happier, more engaged employees mean your company generates great results.

Now imagine a team in which supervisors talk about building Employee Engagement but in reality are simply pushing people without providing support, guiding them, or taking an interest in their personal and career development.

Unhappy and disengaged employees lead to poor results.

> Happier, more engaged employees = great results

> Unhappy and disengaged employees = poor results

TAKE ACTION NOW!

Write down 5 ways you could make your team members happier:

1. _____
_____
_____

2. _____
_____
_____

3. _____
_____
_____

4. _____
_____
_____

5. _____
_____
_____

Tactic #46

Attract the Right Mix

Have a balanced team, with complementary skills, knowledge and personalities

Attract the right people. Note that I didn't say the best people! Depending on your personality, you, the entrepreneur, might want either top players (for whom you must be prepared to pay the price), or a team of low-cost employees. Neither extreme is ideal. Not all jobs require super knowledge and super personality so hiring Superstars exclusively makes no sense. Conversely, prioritizing low cost above everything else will only attract poorly skilled and poorly qualified people.

There are three types of people:

- A-Players are the Superstars, the overachievers, the best candidates, the highest performers;
- B-Players are the average, but acceptable performers;
- C-Players are sub-standard performers.

Having a mix of A- and B-Players is ideal. Have A-Players for the key positions within your company and choose B-Players for the rest. This represents the best skill / cost mix. Plus, these balanced teams are more cohesive and functional than teams in which everybody competes to become Number One. Look for the right person for each job, but also make sure you have complementary skills, knowledge and personalities.

Don't waste Resources on hiring, keeping and putting up with the high demands of an army of super performers. You don't need only generals and captains in your company. Just because you like people like yourself – born leaders – doesn't mean this is a recipe for success. On the other hand, don't keep under-performers (C-Players) unless you see clear potential. Their salaries might be small, but don't forget about your Training costs and, more importantly, the cost of having your Superstars spending time with them instead of delivering to the top of their game for the business.

Now that you understand the Right Mix in terms of performance level, consider what type of person you require for each job and be ready to make some compromises. For the management of marketing activities you want someone who understands marketing (of course) and is good at coordinating and getting the most out of their team members. But for the person responsible for the marketing messages, you may need a creative person, who doesn't necessarily have to be that organized. Compromising on what is not important (organizational skills in the latter example) for each job, each hire, is a great way to get the right people.

You do not need a Superstar to clean the office, but you do want your cleaning staff to have common sense. Why? Because if they don't, you or your personnel manager will spend an enormous amount of time managing this person: showing them where to clean, what to do and how to do it. Constantly checking on the cleaning staff becomes an expensive waste of management's time. Ultimately this may cost you more than paying a better salary to someone who can get on with the job without supervision, think for themselves, and anticipate what your staff need.

The next step is to get your managers to place the right work, in the right quantities, on each employee's plate. **Align the responsibilities of each employee with their skills, as well as their personal interests, talents and career plans.** This way your employees are happier and perform better. Doing less than that (or the complete opposite) is like swimming against the tide.

Here's why you need to do this!

When my son was born, I hired a live-in nanny to help look after him, as well as do the cleaning, cooking and general house-keeping. She was fantastic with my son and excellent at everything else she had to do. She had empathy and she could anticipate our Needs; she would always plan ahead and make sure we had food in the fridge; the house was always tidy and clean. I didn't know what she was doing when, but I knew things were being done. As I did not have to devote any time to managing her, I could concentrate on work.

When I my son was two years old, the nanny had to go back home for a few months, so we hired another (temporary) nanny. She asked for 30% less than the previous one and she ate less, so our overall cost was less. However, though she was fantastic with my son, she was not as organized and prompt with the rest of her tasks.

For example, she was unable to draw up an accurate shopping list for me. She would forget certain items, or put things on the list that we didn't need. The result was that I had to dedicate time to managing her and to keeping an eye on what was going on. Though our costs were lower, I looked forward to the return of our regular nanny so that I could again free up my mind and my time to do what is important: my work. This is where I add the most Value, not in checking to see if we have enough soap in the house until the next shopping trip.

TAKE ACTION NOW!

Think of your core team. Write down 5 capabilities you don't feel are at an optimal level. How can you fill each gap? Write down your ideas below:

1. _____
_____
_____

2. _____
_____
_____

3. _____
_____
_____

4. _____
_____
_____

5. _____
_____
_____

Retain Those Employees Who Fit In

> *Say no – even to highly skilled people – if they don't match your business Culture*

You worked hard to build a company Culture that represents you. You want to maintain this Culture moving forward. Thus, always take into account the personality of the individuals you recruit, and don't compromise on personal traits for skills.

Understand what is important for your company's Culture, and make that a must in new recruits. It could be positive attitude, fun, open, transparent, honest, keen to learn, open to New Ideas, likes challenges, self-starter... whatever it is, make sure that new recruits fit the bill.

Not the right person...

A couple of years ago I got a very senior consultant, extremely skilled and knowledgeable, to join the team and manage the Business Doctor division. Unfortunately, althrough he may have been full of knowledge, he was not willing to share that knowledge with my team. He soon found that none of my staff accepted him, and he had to leave. An unofficial alliance was formed against him and, believe it or not, I took their side. If that consultant was not accepted by my team, it is likely that he would not be liked by my clients or partners. And why would I want to force my team to be managed by someone they don't like? They are wonderful, it is fun to be in the office, they help each other, and I want this open and transparent Culture to be maintained. With the new consultant, I could see a senseless competition being played out among my staff, who would constantly be watching their backs – something I am totally against.

I have a policy that I only offer long-term (unlimited) employment contracts after a three-month trial period. During that initial period I want to test the skills, but also the attitude, the cultural fit, of that potential employee. If there is no match, there is no long-term contract. My team plays a role too: they vote on whether the person should stay. If they say no, it is a no. I never go against their verdict. They spend more time in the office than I do, and will be in the company of the new recruit, more than I will. And they need to be happy.

TAKE ACTION NOW!

Identify 3 people in your company that you don't feel are the right match for the Culture you want to create.

1. _____
_____
_____

2. _____
_____
_____

3. _____
_____
_____

For each person, write down how you could deal with this.

Person 1:
_____
_____
_____

Person 2:
_____
_____
_____

Person 3:
_____
_____
_____

Tactic #48

Get the Most out of Your Team

Make Sure that Your Employees Know What the Company Expects of Them

Show the way... don't just lead the way

Making the best strategies, business plans, job descriptions and internal procedures is a waste of your energy if you take communication for granted. These are just scrap paper if you and your managers are not equally concerned about communicating your Objectives and Expectations in an efficient and consistent manner to everyone within the company.

Business Priorities and Performance Objectives should be on everybody's lips, not lying forgotten in your manager's desk drawer

Knowing the company's Expectations enables people to meet them; getting staff involved in defining the Expectations greatly increases their Motivation. After all, your employees are also human beings with a desire to be a part of something! Okay, you don't have to ask them to set your business's Objectives, but you can (and should) at the very least share the Objectives with them and perhaps ask them to contribute on how to get there.

You might argue: 'But the person loading and unloading the merchandise from the truck doesn't need to contribute ideas on how to create a 30% Sales increase next year!' You are right, but the sales manager should be involved, and there are probably a few other people that you don't currently involve in your planning who could help. As for the worker, he needs to know at least that you want to increase Sales by 30% in the next 12 months, and that you plan to do it by changing A, B, and C, which reflects in his job being slightly adjusted and him loading 15% more trucks.

Business owners often falsely assume that their Expectations are known once they are written in an official document or agreed upon in a formal (or informal) meeting with managers or key people. Even worse, we tend to assume that when we have something in our heads, it has reached everyone else in the company, and they should be executing it.

Chaos or structure? Your choice!

Imagine a marathon in which there are no signs. At the start, people run straight, as is human nature, but what happens when they hit a cross road? They may stop running completely or run off in different directions. Is this how you want your staff to behave? Or would you prefer them to know what they have to do (even when you are not).

Which way?

Now let's take the above example one step further (but assume our marathon route is obvious to the participants): when do the runners get recognition for their efforts? At the finish line. But it is the cheering along the way that Motivates them to reach the finish line!

> *Ask for clear results and constantly show staff how their role (however small) contributes to a larger Business Goal*

TAKE ACTION NOW!

Write down 5 ideas you will implement in the next 30 days that will make it clearer to everyone in the company how your business creates Value for its customers.

1. _____
_____
_____

2. _____
_____
_____

3. _____
_____
_____

4. _____
_____
_____

5. _____
_____
_____

6. _____
_____
_____

Tactic #49 — Get the Most out of Your Team

Ensure Your Employees Know Your Company's Purpose

... and encourage them to constantly seek better ways to create Value for your customers

Do your people know what the Purpose of your business is? It's tempting to give the blunt, if a little cheesy, answer that businesses are here to make profits by means of creating Value for their customers. Ask.com describes the main Purpose of a business organization as 'to serve and gratify its customers whilst making profits. Another Purpose is to achieve the Goals and Objectives as indicated within the organization's Vision Statement with its mission statement indicating how these Goals will be achieved and met'.

But let's dig a bit deeper. Try this quick reality check. How many of your employees do you think can answer the following questions?
- How does the company create Value for the customer and society?
- How does my work generally contribute to this Purpose?
- How does my work today contribute to this Purpose?
- How can I test which part of my job is directly contributing to the big Purpose and which activities are just ineffective routine (i.e. how can I apply the Pareto 80-20 principle)?
- How can I contribute to finding new ways for the business to create more Value for our customers?

Now leave your desk and ask your employees these questions. You might be amazed or shocked by the results.

What are your answers? Needless to say, **if your employees' answers are not in line with yours, you had better spend time with them explaining what the company is all about.**

And if you are employing or planning to hire millenniums, clearly communicating your Purpose is an absolute must, because they seek jobs with purpose.

Is the Purpose clear to you, as the owner of the business?

The first deal my consulting firm closed was the sale of my father's company. He and a friend had 50-50 ownership of an import and distribution company for fishing items. The need to sell the company emerged because it became too complicated to manage. They had 100 employees, and half the market. When I did my due diligence on them to understand the business, I asked my father and his partner what their Strategy was. Neither of them knew. They didn't even know what Strategy meant! So I asked them: 'You sell fishing items. If tomorrow there was an opportunity to make loads of money by selling bikinis, would you sell bikinis?' One said 'yes', the other said 'no'. So not only did they not have a Strategy, they also didn't know what they wanted from this company. Imagine what the employees knew or thought about the company's Purpose...

We at Tooliers have clarified that our purpose is to change the world by empowering entrepreneurs to build Smarter Businesses and by reducing the struggle, stress and frustration amongst small business owners. The entire team has got more interested and committed... simply because it is a cause that we all support. We have been through tough times and we know how it feels to not have enough money to pay the salaries. We also know that each business can have a stable income to cover the basics, when they have a systematic approach. Since we know how painful it is when there is not enough money, not enough time, when clients don't pay on time or at all, and when there are many more challenges we have been through ourselves, each member of our team is fully committed to reducing the struggle amongst small businesses, because we all want to contribute towards improving other people's lives.

My entire team knows that by helping fellow entrepreneurs, our activity has a ripple effect, because our clients make the lives of their clients better. And this is really our supreme motivation.

Same thing. Different approach!

My team had a chat with one of our clients who was very happy that his sales are 15% higher due to our online marketing activities. My colleague who informed me didn't tell me: "Ozana, we are so clever that our strategy increased sales by 15% for client X". He told me: "Ozana, client X is grateful to us for proposing and executing strategy Y, and 3,000 parks in the entire country will look better over the next two years (our client sells equipment for parks, gardens and other green spaces). He achieved a 15% increase in sales."

See the difference? He didn't focus on the sales increase, but on the effect that our client has on his client's lives. And this makes everyone happier.

What's your bigger reason for being in business?

I have to admit that it wasn't easy for me to articulate our company's purpose. It took me a very long time to nail it and to be able to express it succinctly.

If you have the same challenge, you may want to consider the 7 WHYs Bootcamp™ I run for driven entrepreneurs, where we work on reconnecting with the business and discovering the essence the business which is then put together into your key powerful messages.

Check it out: **www.ozanagiusca.com/7-whys**

TAKE ACTION NOW!

Write down 5 ideas you will implement in the next 30 days that will make it clearer to everyone in the company how your business creates Value for its customers.

1. _____
_____
_____

2. _____
_____
_____

3. _____
_____
_____

4. _____
_____
_____

5. _____
_____
_____

Tactic #50

Implement a Massive Action Plan

Set Goals and Actions in those areas important for your business's growth

Massive Action Plan (MAP) is, as the term suggests, about planning massive action. You start with your Vision and with the End Goal. What do you want to achieve in a year or in a three-year period? Based on your overall Vision, get your first year Goal. Decide which areas of your business you will be working on to achieve your Goal. For each area you need to set Specific Goals, and break them down into Quarterly Goals. Then, assign responsibilities to your team and get on with things.

When you develop your MAP consider the following:

1. **Vision.** This is where you see your company getting to in the long term.

2. **Purpose.** State clearly why you are doing what you are doing (see Tactic #49 'Ensure Your Employees Know Your Company's Purpose'). Why does your team want to be involved? Their Purpose should be included in your MAP.

3. **Consequences.** Include what happens if you fail to achieve the Objectives. Some people are Motivated by pleasure achieving (the Goal), others are Motivated by pain (avoiding failure). Include both elements to Motivate your entire team.

4. **Goals.** Do the high-level planning with your senior staff. Select the areas you want to work on during the year, and set Goals for each area. Then set Quarterly Goals for each area. Ensure that the person in charge of each area you choose to work on takes part in these discussions.

5. **Activities.** This is the 'what', 'whom' and 'by when': specific activities undertaken by certain members of your team, to be done by specific deadlines. Work on each area separately, and involve as many of your staff as possible in MAP-ing the area that is of concern to them.

Break down your Main Goals into Smaller Goals and then into digestible activities

Do it like this!

Let's assume that, as the business owner, your overall Goal is to increase profits by 50% within a year. You need to identify how you can achieve this Goal. Areas that you may want to consider are:

- **Sales.** *You want to increase Sales by 50%.*
- *Internal operations. You want to be more efficient internally, and decrease costs by 10%.*
- **Motivation of employees.** *You want to increase Motivation of your staff, so they are more efficient and produce better results. Let's say you want to increase the level of performance by 10%.*
- **Financing.** *You need to finance the growth. If you grow your Sales by 50% you may need to stock up on raw materials, or products, or even extend customer credit. So let's say you need additional finance*

Each area of focus (see examples above) has its own Objective. In your MAP, you break Goals for each area into Quarterly Goals. And then you set actions to achieve the Quarterly Goals.

Let's look at Sales growth, the first area you want to work on. Your first Quarter Goal is to establish the System you use to approach more customers. Your sales manager should be part of this discussion. Activities or solutions might include setting up a Partnership for new distribution channels, or simply organizing your internal sales team to be more efficient.

Let's say you agree to prioritize the latter. A simple way of increasing the efficiency of your sales staff is to remove their other responsibilities and allow them to sell only. If they are spending 40% of their time on preparing contracts, issuing invoices or drawing up other post-sale documents, this is 40% less efficiency in Sales. In other words, they only work at 60% efficiency. Once you have removed their admin work, they can spend 40% more time on Sales – and you should see a 40% increase in Sales. How do you remove the admin work from the salespeople? You simply employ another admin person to deal with Sales-related admin / paperwork.

When you then set up the Sales actions you may want to invite your entire sales team to contribute. They may bring New Ideas or approaches. And even if they don't bring any brilliant ideas, you still want them involved, as you want them to take ownership of the plan, and be really focused on implementing it.

CATEGORY	VISION	GENERAL PORPOSE	1 YEAR GOAL	Q1 GOALS	Q2 GOALS	Q3 GOALS	Q4 GOALS
• ___	• ___	• ___	• ___	• ___	• ___	• ___	• ___
• ___	• ___	• ___	• ___	• ___	• ___	• ___	• ___
• ___	• ___	• ___	• ___	• ___	• ___	• ___	• ___

Have your relevant staff contribute to drafting their share of the MAP, rather than simply communicating it to them

TAKE ACTION NOW!

Write down your overall one-year Goal, the reason you want to achieve this Goal, and what happens if you don't achieve it.

Goal: _____

Reason: _____

Consequence: _____

Write down the areas you will be working on to achieve your Goal for next year:

1. _____
_____
_____

2. _____
_____
_____

3. _____
_____
_____

4. _____
_____
_____

5. _____
_____
_____

Share Short-Term and Medium-Term Goals with Everyone in the Company

You have a Vision for your company. You know where you want to get to. You may also know how to get there. But do your employees know?

> *Get your relevant staff involved when you plan each Area of Focus*

We already saw the value of internal communication in Tactic #48 'Ensure Your Employees Know What the Company Expects of Them'. Now, it is your turn to communicate Goals by setting Specific Objectives based on your Vision – and as you set them in your MAP in Tactic #50 'Implement a Massive Action Plan'. Starting with the aim or Vision in mind, go backwards, and set Specific Objectives for each quarter, based on the yearly Objectives. (For tips on setting these Objectives, see Tactic #52 'Use S-M-A-R-T Objectives…').

Next, assign tasks and responsibilities to people based on this medium- to long-term view. Regardless of how well organized you are and how clearly you have set your short-term and medium-term Objectives, you have to communicate these to your team – in particular to your managers, who should then communicate with their team members. Your managers should also set their own short- and medium-term Objectives, which should then be reflected in their team's everyday activities. Of course, Objectives have to be relevant to the employee's skill-set and the company's Vision.

> *You will achieve best results when your staff feel they are part of the business's Vision*

By establishing medium- and short-term Priorities in line with the overall business Strategy and Vision, you give your staff an overall understanding, a clear direction and a Purpose for their day-to-day efforts. In essence, you are facilitating Goal Alignment, which is critical for business success. This ensures that each person within your organization can see the direction for the business and knows how their job fits in the 'big picture'.

By allowing managers to access and view the Goals of other departments, your organization can greatly reduce redundancy while finding better ways for staff departments to support each other.

With everyone working together toward the same Objectives, your company will execute its Strategy faster, with more flexibility and adaptability. Essentially, Goal Alignment strengthens your leadership and creates organizational agility by allowing managers to:

- achieve what is important, by focusing employees' efforts on your company's most important Goals;
- execute and deliver quickly, by understanding clearly responsibilities associated with Specific Goals;
- increase Accountability by assigning measurable, articulated Goals visible within the entire company

Seeing the bigger picture!

One construction worker can think that he is digging a hole in the ground, while another knows that he is contributing to laying the foundation of the greatest highway on Earth. The work is the same, the mindset entirely different. Sharing with your team your current road map to making your Vision real helps your employees see the larger picture and understand the connection between their everyday chores and the final destination.

The employee buys into the business's vision

As a business owner, it is your responsibility to ensure your team leaders, managers and coordinators understand the difference between drilling a hole and laying the foundation for a great piece of work. It is also up to you to ensure that your leadership team is able to make people feel that they are part of colossal projects rather than simply overwhelm them with demanding and meaningless tasks.

TAKE ACTION NOW!

Write down your overall Goal:
_____
_____
_____

Write down your Mini-Goals. Once these are clear to you, involve your team to ensure these Goals are clear in their minds too. By doing this, they see how their tasks are linked to the business's Goals.

1. _____
_____
_____

2. _____
_____
_____

3. _____
_____
_____

4. _____
_____
_____

5. _____
_____
_____

Tactic #52 — Get the Most out of Your Team

Set S-M-A-R-T Objectives...

> ...and be smart enough to know that no matter how S-M-A-R-T your Objectives, they might require reconsideration

We have discussed that you set Goals in your MAP. Those Goals are in fact translated into Objectives, which you have to ensure are S-M-A-R-T. If you don't already know it, here is the S-M-A-R-T framework:

- **Specific:** Well-defined to inform employees exactly what is expected, when, and how much. With Specific Goals, managers can easily measure progress toward Goal completion.
- **Measurable:** Provide milestones to track progress and Motivate employees toward achievement.
- **Attainable:** Success needs to be achievable with effort by an average employee, not too high or too low.
- **Relevant:** Focus on the greatest impact to the overall company Strategy.
- **Time-bound:** Establish enough time to achieve the Goal, but not too much time to undermine performance. Goals without deadlines tend to be overtaken by day-to-day crises.

And most importantly, hold people Accountable for achieving the Goals. The easiest way to accomplish this is by involving them in the setting up their own Goals and Objectives. Every time you embark on a new project or a new initiative, go through the S-M-A-R-T process to clarify the Objectives, based on the over-riding Goals. The clearer this is for everybody, the higher the chances of the Goal being achieved. Those who are not involved in setting the

> *Be smart. Have S-M-A-R-T objectives.*

direction in your company, should at the very least be informed about your Goals and their Objectives. Use this framework at the highest level, as well as for small projects. If you are about to launch a new product, this should be planned within the S-M-A-R-T framework too.

This is how it is (and isn't) done!

S-M-A-R-T Objectives	Objectives that are not S-M-A-R-T
Complete at least 25 cold calls to qualified prospects by September 1, 2010.	Conduct as many Sales calls as possible as soon as possible.
Increase Sales of Waffle Wraps to chain grocery stores by 8% over last year by December 31, 2010.	Sell as many Waffle Wraps as possible this year.
Convert 33% of leads to customers within 30 days of initial contract.	Convert some leads every day so that you always have new customers.
Follow up with every prospect and customer within 48 hours of Sales call.	Follow up with every prospect and customer after a Sales call.

To help set S-M-A-R-T Objectives ask yourself and your team:

- What are we going to do, with whom or for whom?
- How will this be done and what strategies will be used?
- Why is this important to do?
- Is the Objective understood?
- Is the Objective described with action verbs?
- Who is going to be responsible for what and do we need anyone else to be involved?
- Where will this happen?

- When do we want this to be completed?
- What needs to happen?
- Is the outcome clear?
- Will this Objective lead to desired results?

TAKE ACTION NOW!

Write down 5 S-M-A-R-T Objectives for your business:

1. _____
_____
_____

2. _____
_____
_____

3. _____
_____
_____

4. _____
_____
_____

5. _____
_____
_____

Tactic #53   Get the Most out of Your Team

Train Your Sales Staff Exceptionally Well

Top Training leads to better Skills and – equally importantly – higher Motivation

As the business owner, you probably sold your product or service initially yourself – or you are still doing so. You, or someone else, must have mastered such Sales, or your business wouldn't exist. You need that Knowledge to be transferred to your sales force and you (or whoever else performed the initial Sales) need to Train your current sales force. **It is not enough to tell them what to do. You need to show them how to do it. It is best if you can demonstrate how to each of your salespeople.** Give them the process and tools they need, whether the steps to take, or a pitch or presentation style, or other materials they may need. Answer all their questions. Go into the field with them and check how they are doing. Observe and help them improve. You are their coach, so it is entirely your responsibility to Train them and to ensure they know what they are doing.

Train your sales force and you will earn their loyalty

Record your Training sessions. You can use these recordings again with them in future, or with new recruits. Other people within your company will eventually use these recordings too.

There is never 'too much Training'! Perform frequent Training! As their coach, you need to have regular meetings with sales staff, to constantly improve what they do. Observe what the Best Performers do, and get the others to follow suit. Of course, you can use outside Trainers, if you prefer, but make a point of getting involved too.

And if you don't know how to do it…

> *Get all your sales people together, look at the Best Performer(s) and ask them to explain to the team what they do and how they do it, so the others copy what works for the Best Performer(s). You are the facilitator, if nothing else. You need to ensure that step-by-step actions are being taught by your Best Performer(s).*

TAKE ACTION NOW!

Write down 5 ideas you will implement in the next 30 days to Train your staff better, as well as to improve your company's Training System.

1. _____
_____
_____

2. _____
_____
_____

3. _____
_____
_____

4. _____
_____
_____

5. _____
_____
_____

Regularly Monitor the Motivation of Your Staff

Keep in touch with how your people perform and how engaged they are. Being aware is the minimum you can do

The success of your business is highly dependent on the performance of your staff. And their performance is dependent on their Motivation.

As a small business owner, you don't really need complicated KPIs and sophisticated Performance Management Systems to know who is delivering and who isn't. Nor do you need cutting-edge Employee Engagement Surveys to ascertain how excited your staff is to work for you. Just go out there and see for yourself. Track Employee Motivation through observation of how enthusiastic they are about arriving at work, interacting with colleagues and engaging in activities to which they are assigned. You may also like to teach your managers to note everyone's reactions when undertaking a new project.

Keeping people engaged is most often as simple as eliminating certain tasks and removing their pain, rather than performing miracles.

I take time to talk regularly to each of my employees. (Granted, I don't have hundreds of them – yet.) I do this because I want to know how they feel about working with the company, what they like, what they don't like, what they expect, and where they see themselves. Such discussions help me paint a picture of the company that I can't see by myself. These talks also help make my organization more efficient as many of the best suggestions come from my staff.

Now we're talking!

When I was still testing Business Lens™ (our toolkit to identify what you don't do well or enough of in your business), I had everyone in the company fill in the survey (a series of multiple choice questions). I then had the results centralized into an Excel file, with one column showing the grades of each employee, though I did not know which grades belonged to whom. I noticed that most of the grades were in line with my expectations and relatively close one to another – except for one, which was way below the others. I knew immediately whom these grades belonged to: a colleague who was often moaning and complaining. His internal unhappiness was reflected in those grades, and in the distance between himself and the rest of the team. He wasn't happy with us anymore, so he saw everything in a negative light. That same employee had produced great results for us in the past, but he simply wasn't motivated any more to work with us. Doing an exercise like this can help you spot those employees who have problems in or with your company, or it can confirm something you already suspected.

Motivate your staff to achieve maximum performance

The fact that an employee isn't performing according to your expectations may not be his problem, but yours. Every time you are tempted to let someone go, use it as an opportunity to look in the mirror and learn. Somehow you either hired or promoted someone who failed to perform according to expectations. Ask yourself: how did this happen and how can I keep it from happening again? Be careful also to distinguish between valuable employees who are simply being misused or are misplaced, and those employees who are detrimental to your business's health, as a result of poor work ethic, apathy or overall lack of interest.

Maintaining appropriate levels of Motivation, satisfaction and performance among your work force is an on-going process. Don't let measuring employee sentiments be a one-time activity. Add it to your list of annual tasks through which you demonstrate to employees that you are genuinely concerned about their work life.

I lost it

After 6 years of working for my company, one of my core team members left. Somehow I knew this was going to happen. I could feel it. But I didn't know what to do. I was aware that I had focused on developing a few more products and for that reason I was almost absent from my team's life. I trusted them to do a great job and I concentrated on what I'd set myself to do, which was great because I could develop those new products in record time, given their complexity.

What happened was that my team felt somehow abandoned. They were still communicating, doing what they were supposed to do, and everything was fine on the surface. But over six months, those employees who needed me there, simply to gather everyone together during our Monday morning meetings and coordinate the discussion, felt my absence. And within a few months one team member left because she no longer felt she belonged in our company.

The conclusion is that while some people don't need any emotional connection and support, others do. And if that support is not there, they'll look for it elsewhere.

Would you like to know how I got to know this? I asked my colleague if there was anything that I should have done differently so she would not have left.

TAKE ACTION NOW!

Write down 5 ideas you will implement in the next 30 days to ensure you monitor and increase the Motivation of your staff:

1. _____
_____
_____

2. _____
_____
_____

3. _____
_____
_____

4. _____
_____
_____

5. _____
_____
_____

Tactic #55

Align the Individual Goals of Your Staff with Company Goals

Try to accommodate your staff's wishes where possible. An employee might want to leave the office at 3pm on Fridays and be happy to make up for this by putting in an extra hour per day from Monday to Thursday. Why not give this to them? Ask your employees what they want... and you will be surprised by what you hear! Often they don't want the things you think they do (like tons of extra money or fancy perks).

When I did the Massive Action Plan (MAP) for my consulting company, I had my whole team contribute. One of the directions in the MAP was Tooliers®. When we filled in the Purpose (i.e. why we want Tooliers® to be a success), I was amazed to discover that my reasons were different from those of my team. There is a clear overlap, but some people have strong reasons centered on things like developing themselves, showing the world what we can do, helping lots of other small businesses do better business... the list goes on. Money was not the main driver for any of my staff!

How can you find out your employees' Goals? You ask them. Some don't have any, or simply haven't thought of their Goals and many may require more time to reflect on it – don't rush them. They need to understand what they really want. They also need to know what they want from your company. It can help to ask them the following question: 'Imagine you are walking along the street when a genie crosses your path. He asks you to tell him three wishes and promises to make them come true. What are those wishes?'. Don't promise to fulfill them! Use this game to understand where your staff are coming from, and to meet them there, where possible.

> *Fulfill your employees' wishes and they will be more dedicated to your business*

Now we're talking!

*At some point I was in a rush to get **Business Lens™**, out on the market which was down to one person to finish. When I asked her to give it to me to finalize, so that we could send it to the programmers within the deadline, she told me she would prefer to do overtime and finish it. She wanted to feel that she had accomplished something. Of course I let her complete the job, even though it might have been quicker had I finished it myself. I gave her what she wanted and she felt good about her achievement. Plus, I could use that time to work on something else.*

Happy employees are more engaged and loyal and more productive in the short, medium and long term. **Investing in your staff's happiness by taking the time to know them and by getting them involved in the right projects pays off (literally).** Just think about all the recruiting, training and integration costs you avoid by keeping and developing your existing taskforce.

Being in touch with your employees and constantly understanding them, supporting them, and checking in with them is part of your job. Yes, you can have someone deal with your employees, you can have a manager running the company, but you still have to dedicate time to meet your employees from time to time, for a one-on-one chat. In other words, those working meetings or conversations don't count here. What you really want is to identify if your employees' objectives have changed, and make some adjustments in the way they work, what they do, what they get out of the relationship with your company, so that they are happy working for you.

Why do you need such periodic talks with your key staff? Well, because as time goes by, people change. Their circumstances change. They may have a new baby, or get married, or someone close to them dies... which makes them change their priorities, and have different needs. Therefore, they may expect the company to give them something slightly different, to make their lives more manageable. And in most cases, it is easy to accommodate what your employees want, as long as you talk to them regularly, so you find out what it is.

Don't expect your employees to ask you for what they want. Meet them, find out what it is and give it to them if possible— and of course, if it is reasonable. This way you prevent unfortunate situations where your key people leave, and you also maintain their high level of motivation and commitment. Simply because you care for your staff, and they feel it!

> *Don't expect your employees to ask you for what they want. Be pro-active!*

TAKE ACTION NOW!

Ask your staff what their Goals are and why they are working for your company. Write down 5 of these Goals and reasons and how you will try to fulfill those that are reasonable.

1. _____
   _____
   _____

2. _____
   _____
   _____

3. _____
   _____
   _____

4. _____
   _____
   _____

5. _____
   _____
   _____

Tactic #56

Get the Most out of Your Team

Don't Use Money to Motivate Your Staff

Pay your staff fairly, no question about it, but don't use money as the sole Motivation for your employees to perform. Money is there to ensure the comfort of your employees, but Motivation is obtained mainly through non-monetary means.

People like to be treated fairly and, from time to time, it is a good idea to give them more than that. Giving the royal treatment always works like a charm to rally people around your mission. The trouble is everyone has their own idea about what the royal treatment constitutes and, too often, the manager's idea of this is quite different from that of the employee. Never make the mistake of assuming that a raise or a bonus will do the trick for everyone. In fact, it can be difficult to know what makes certain employees tick. Some might react positively to having more freedom and enjoying flexible working hours. Others might be more excited about being publicly praised. Many would appreciate it and give more to their employers if the company would make their lives as working parents easier.

Just because you are driven by a dream of becoming a millionaire, or a billionaire, doesn't mean that your employees share that dream. The magic solution here is that there is no magic solution. **You have to listen, observe, bear in mind individual differences and then be sure to give people what makes them tick.**

Some ideas to implement and increase Motivation

- *Give your employees tremendous freedom, such as planning their week as they consider effective or trying their ideas for new products or simply trying new ways of doing things.*
- *Apply flexible working hours, flexible start and end times.*
- *Consider what each member of your team likes and is good at when you divide responsibilities.*
- *Offer 'concierge' services to your employees, whereby you contract someone to do personal jobs like taking clothes to the dry-cleaners,*

picking up a parcel, or even driving their kids to school.
- *Give performance recognition in public. Make a habit of praising one employee every day!*
- *Have easy, regular conversations with your people.*
- *Show a natural interest in people.*
- *Say 'thank you' and give praise regularly.*
- *Give credit where it is due.*
- *Treat everyone equally and fairly.*
- *Always keep the promises you make – or don't make them.*
- *Delegate responsibility wherever you can, with guidance.*
- *Challenge your employees.*
- *Coach, support and guide your staff to their success.*

Still not convinced? Do you know it costs three times the salary of an existing employee to replace that employee? Think about the time it takes to find and recruit a new employee and the cost of training that employee to the same level of productivity. All the more reason to find out what Motivates your employees...

TAKE ACTION NOW!

IIdentify 5 areas you would like to measure in the next year. For each area, write down how you will measure it:

1. _____
_____
_____

2. _____
_____
_____

3. _____
_____
_____

4. _____
_____
_____

5. _____
_____
_____

Smart Business System™

In my experience, which includes being responsible for increasing the profits of 100 companies over the past three years – in some cases doubling and even tripling profits – I've noticed that most people running a small business or working alone, face 7 main challenges to increasing sales.

Many believe their lack of further success is due to legislation, taxation, red tape, banks not lending or the government not helping small businesses, but the truth is there are 7 challenges that are within your control to overcome, which makes all the difference.

It is important to understand these challenges, to identify which ones you are facing and then to use the very best system to overcome your specific challenges.

Because I also faced these challenges, specifically when I was struggling to sell with Tooliers *(www.tooliers.com)*, I have developed the **Smarter Business System™**, which is our battle-tested solution for achieving objectives faster.

My team and I have been using this system on a daily basis. Initially we kept it for ourselves and for a select group of clients. Now, we share it freely with fellow entrepreneurs, experts and driven professionals who want more.

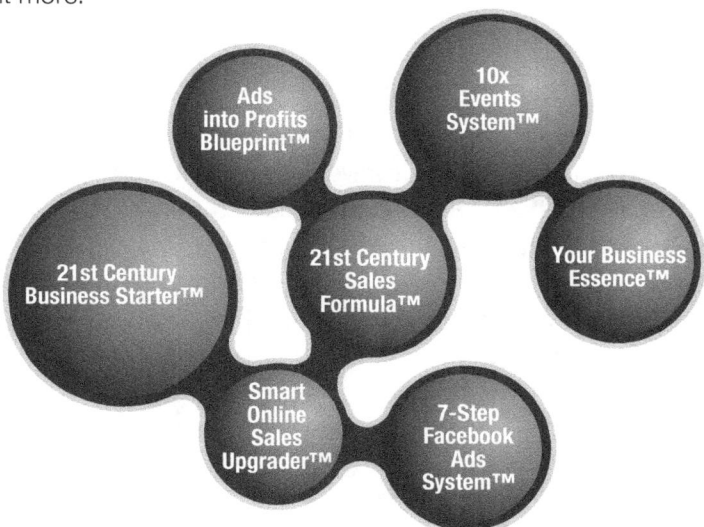

Smart Business System™

It is my pleasure to invite you to my online or live Master Classes in which I detail the system and its components.

Join me wherever it is convenient for you. Select from the events listed at **www.ozanagiusca.com/my-events** whatever best suits you and your needs. Some events are free and some require an investment.

Below I share more about the 7 challenges that block the growth of most businesses as well as the sub-system I have developed to overcome each challenge.

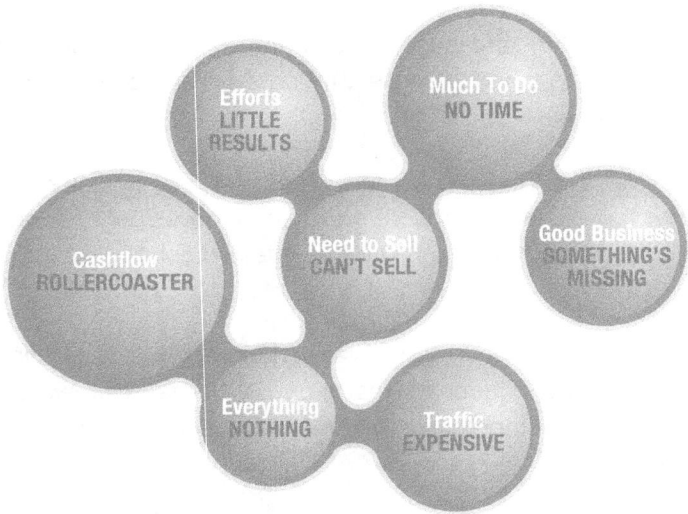

Challenge #1

Small business owners **want to sell more and have a stable, solid income**. Increasing the sales involves having a saleable product or service, a sales system and a way to feed this system with potential leads. Because there are various potential issues that need to be addressed before a business really takes off and grows exponentially, the **cash flow of most entrepreneurs is often like a rollercoaster** (sometimes up, more often down).

Too many meetings end up being a waste of time. Networking may be okay for social reasons, but few people buy from those they meet at events. A potential client suddenly goes cold... and whatever we do, it seems that people are simply no longer interested in buying.

Today, **people don't buy the way they used to**.

Due to the technology developments and the internet, the way people buy has changed. Which means that if you want to sell more, you also need to change your approach.

You need to adapt your business to the current reality. This is having the 21st Century Business Approach, the 21st Century Business Marketing Methods, and the 21st Century Business Essentials (this is not about the essentials in your business, which I am sure you have, but about the essentials that your business needs to give to you, its owner), because business as usual, as in the past, is no longer an option.

The key words here are Customer's Journey, a term that many experts talk about, but which is not understood and leveraged as it should be. This is about you **building a number of pre-programmed interactions with your potential clients, so you take them from "I don't know you" to buying from you and even recommending you to others**.

In most cases, such a 'journey' doesn't happen naturally. You need to engineer it, so your potential clients take the right steps (depending on where they are in relation to wanting your type of product or service) towards you and only you.

In order to build the road for such a journey, you need the 21st Century Business MAP.

21st Century Business MAP™

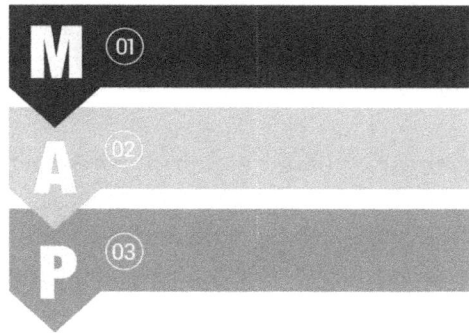

Deploying this system is the way to not only stay in business long term, but to thrive and generate increasing cash flow.

We are talking about combining online with offline activities, about talking to the potential client more but mainly in an automated or semi-automated manner, so you really leverage what you have and know so you achieve smarter profits faster.

I discuss this new approach and how to position your company, product or service and how to build your Customers' Journeys during the Smart Business Accelerator™ *(www.ozanagiusca.com/kim-en)*, strategic workshop over two days.

If you want to be in full control of your business; if you are fed up with trying various approaches which waste your money and time only to bring stress and frustration; and if you are committed now to investing to transform and scale your business, to maximize your profits and increase your impact so you achieve YOUR objectives, then I'm here to support you!

I invite you to join me for my next workshop where we will plan your Smarter Business *(www.ozanagiusca.com/kim-en)*.

Challenge #2

Before they started working with us, our clients were doing various activities, trying to sell to as many people as possible, but only getting a few clients.

I often see entrepreneurs busily developing a new product, serving existing clients, trying to source extra help, doing the admin tasks and even taking the trash out. They are constantly busy, feeling overwhelmed by how much they have to do… but what progress do they actually make?

For these entrepreneurs, I have developed the **Smart Online Sales Upgrader™**, to enable you to get more and better clients fast. Because generating business online can be done on auto or semi-auto pilot and when the system is deployed correctly, you have more time to do what you really love.

See in the illustration below how you can deploy this method to build your own system, to generate business online and have a constant and predictable cash flow.

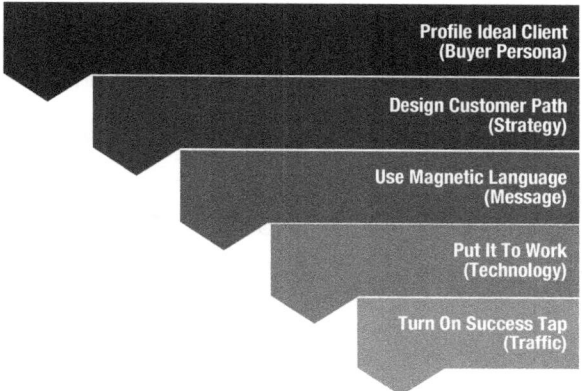

Under our guidance, participants in our Smart Online Sales Bootcamp™ *(www.ozanagiusca.com/sos-bootcamp-en)* achieve in two days what they have struggled to do on their own for years!

This method works because it has been tested on more than 400 entrepreneurs in most industries, ranging from professional services (consultants, coaches, experts) to manufacturing and retail.

The secret here is CLARITY. And to get clarity you need to go through a series of questions and, of course, answer them systematically, on paper.

Challenge #3

The majority of small businesses want more traffic in their store (online or offline) or visiting their website. Traffic is expensive, though, and they can't afford to waste resources on promotional activities that don't lead to sales.

We've figured that Facebook is the best platform right now to get traffic. It works for all businesses, but only when deployed correctly. If you are wondering if Facebook Ads are for you (i.e. investing in promotion on Facebook), join my next online Master Class *(www.ozanagiusca.com/facebook-ads-why-en)* on this subject.

Smart Business System™

We have developed the 7-Step Smart Business Facebook Ads System which we'll present during this Master Class. Simply go to **www.ozanagiusca.com/facebook-ads-system-en**, register, attend, take notes and implement.

We tested and tested... invested $100,000+ in our own campaigns and helped 300+ clients run profitable ads campaigns.

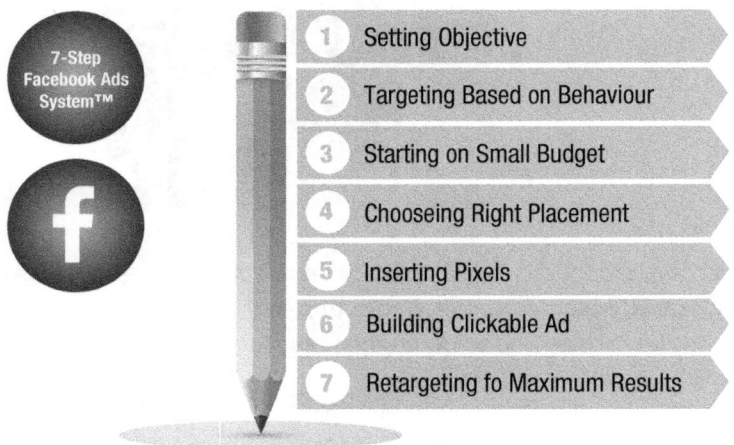

Challenge #4

Many people running their own show, be it a one-man venture or an established business, **need to sell but don't know how**. The truth is that selling is a skill you can learn. What's interesting is that most of our clients don't want to even consider taking sales courses. Because, just as they don't like others trying to sell to them, they know their potential clients don't want to hear from another pushy sales person. Besides, we set up our businesses based on our passion, because we want to help others and change the world, and we don't want to sound like second-hand car salesmen!

Many of my clients find themselves in a catch 22: they know their product or service is excellent but clients only realize and appreciate the value once they've experienced the product. Unable to clearly explain this amazing value to their potential clients, they have to constantly decrease their price just to make a sale.

The solution is the **21st Century Sales Formula™**, which is about helping your potential clients in advance so you show them, before asking for the sale, that you are the right person to help them.

The secret is to do it in such a way that you **create interest for your product or service so you don't even have to "sell" for a sale to happen**.

Imagine your best clients coming to you and begging you to sell to them!

Join my next Master Class on How to Accelerate Your Sales *(www.ozanagiusca.com/accelerate-sales)* to discover how easy this is. And yes, this is exactly what I do – I create interest and earn the trust of potential clients (like you) by offering real help in my Master Classes without any sales talk.

The more value you create in your marketplace, the more offers you can make. And of course, the more offers you make, the more sales you can achieve.

21st Century Sales Formula™

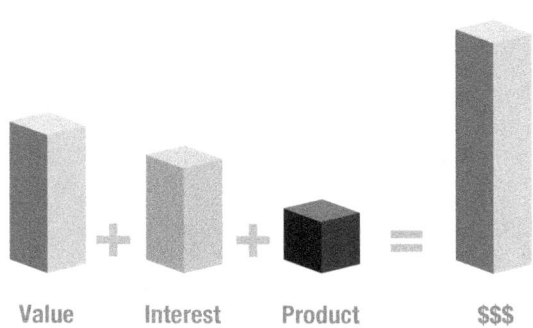

Value   Interest   Product $$$

Challenge #5

Most people in business have invested money, time and a lot of efforts in promotion, but the results are far from satisfying. This is because many tactics have been used in isolation without a strategy to back them up.

If you feel you have this challenge, then I highly encourage you to discover my Ads into Profit Blueprint™, where you can get answers to your burning questions about advertising, and more importantly, where you can ask more questions to help you get the RIGHT answers. Yes, it is only when you ask yourself the right questions that you can get helpful answers, so you can really get a good return on their promo budget.

Access Ads into Profits Master Class *(www.ozanagiusca.com/turn-ads-into-profitable-customers)* to get the right answers to the right questions.

Most entrepreneurs gain business in the traditional way. What you'll understand is how to expand beyond what you do well and break through the current sales figure, by adding other products, services, actions.

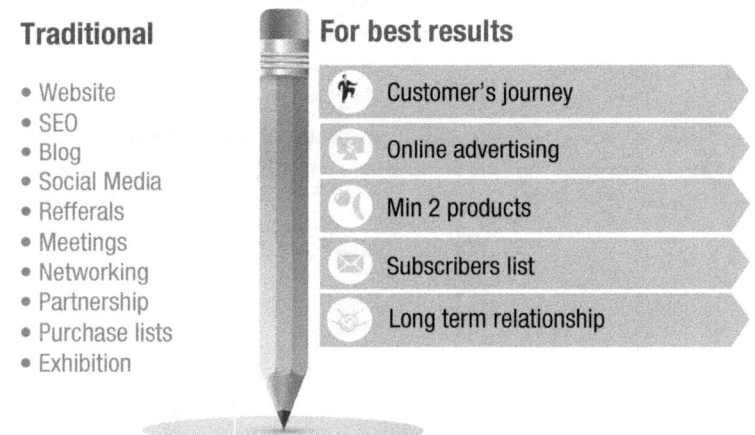

Traditional
- Website
- SEO
- Blog
- Social Media
- Refferals
- Meetings
- Networking
- Partnership
- Purchase lists
- Exhibition

For best results
- Customer's journey
- Online advertising
- Min 2 products
- Subscribers list
- Long term relationship

Challenge #6

Most people in business have a lot to do and not enough time to do it! They wish the working day had 48 hours so they could hold more meetings with potential clients and show their product to more people; to ultimately increase their sales and profits.

Well, there is a way for you to have 50 to 500 sales conversations in an hour or so. If you're asking yourself how this is possible, the **10x Events System™** *(www.ozanagiusca.com/10x-sales-bootcamp-en)* is for you.

Instead of giving away valuable information about your product or service during a sales conversation, share it in an educational or fun context, when your potential clients WANT to hear you talk about your offering.

The benefit of selling at events is that it is the most efficient way to sell, while getting your potential clients to love you for the experience and information you provide.

What do I mean by 'events'? It could be a workshop, a webinar, a series of online videos, a sampling / tasting or networking event, even a fashion show.

As you become closer to being an important player in your niche, you need to consider selling from the stage/ via events. This is not just for experts and trainers. Our clients who have introduced events in their marketing and selling activities include fashion, car repair, consultants, kids development, agricultural equipment, even doctors.

Of course, we are not talking about just any event! There is a way to hold events of the highest quality, which I share with you in the **10x Events System™** *(www.ozanagiusca.com/10x-sales-bootcamp-en)*.

Challenge #7

Whether an established business or a newcomer, we all want to make more money. For some, money is a means to living the desired lifestyle, and for others it's a means to show they've achieved a lot and gained the appreciation and respect they deserve.

The challenges are that due to daily activities, and fires that need to be put out, entrepreneurs forget about their destination and most often behave as if lost in a dark forest.

In addition, in a world with so many people trying to sell so much it is difficult to grab your clients' attention. In a world where it is hard to get the right employees, and where communication is so important... it is not easy to 'construct' the right messages that attract the right people. You need to formulate your messages, with a view to ensuring that they are short and to the point, but most importantly, that they get to the heart of your potential clients. Such communication depends on the clarity you have about yourself and your business, and the connection between the two.

Unless you have a set of key messages that you and your team consistently use, you are just another seller, talking in generic terms like most people. This means you are forced to keep your price to a minimum, rather than getting paid for the real value you provide.

In other words, you need to carefully draft your key messages to use as your introduction, as a conversation opener or even on stage when you speak in front of more people. In order to get it right, you need to go to the essence of your business.

This is YOUR job!

No external consultants can come up with your key messages because they have to represent you. And the good news is that when you work on identifying such messages, you'll reconnect with your business and fall in love with it all over again.

The outcome is the right foundation for your communication, and you'll really become unstoppable and truly fulfilled when you answer the 7 WHY-based questions shown in the illustration below.

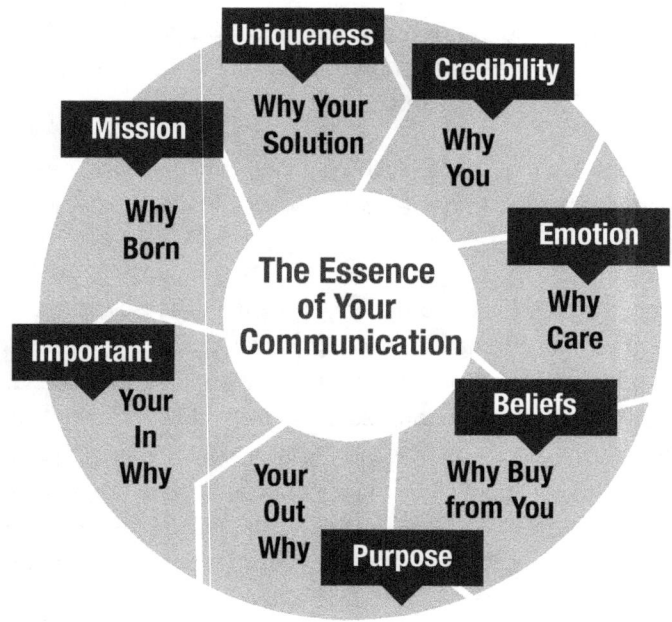

Big companies spent tens of thousands of dollars to identify their key messages. We've created a process to help you distill your key messages without spending an arm and a leg.

Would you like to overcome any of these challenges?

Then I invite you to join my **Smart Business Accelerator™** *(www.ozanagiusca.com/kim-en)* to discover how to build your Smarter Business, your business anchored in the current reality, and adapted to your current needs, aligned to your heart, so you feel in control and get to your destination faster.

Let's spend two days together, and you will

- Evaluate your growth opportunities to unleash the full potential of your business

- Eliminate time wasters, so you really focus on what is most important for you

Leave this workshop with clarity, ways to upgrade your business and a plan of action so you achieve your objectives faster.

Bonus: Love Letter

More value to you

I write about giving more Value than anticipated to your clients, about amazing your customers, about giving something for free. Here, it is my freebie to wow you.

Following, you will find the easieast way to come up with your marketing strategy. I give you the tool so you define your marketing strategy in 30 minutes. The tool is in the form of a letter you write to yourself as if it was written by your Best Customer. I call it 'Love Letter' because it shows the love your customers have to your company. It looks like a testimonial, but it is much more than that. Fill in the blanks. The point of this letter is to help you really understand your business, and what matters for your business's success. It looks like a testimonial, but it is way more than that. Once this letter sounds right, you know the recipe for your business's success. You have more clarity about your own business. You just need to execute correctly (You can do that by applying the 101 tactics in this book).

Below you will find a template for your Love Letter, as well as the letter I wrote for Tooliers®. This helps me 'name' my Persona, the benefits of my product (both logical and emotional), the impact my product has on customers' lives, how to find our customers, what to use to find customers, what I want my customers journey to be, how to ask them to provide recommendations, and more.

This template is your Strategy in a nutshell! And yes, you can use this to get inspiration for what you want your (real) client testimonials to look like.

I challenge you to fill in the blanks for your business. If you want the original, so you don't have to type up the template, visit ***www.ozanagiusca.com/love-letter/*** and grab your copy for free.

Love Letter Template

Dear **[Company Name]**,

My name is **[Persona's name]** and I must tell you I love your **[product type]** and I feel compelled to tell you my story.

I am a **[business type / life or lifestyle role]** who **[problem / passion statement]**. Thing is, that **[impact of pain / passion to life]**.

But **[Product Name]** changed my life.

Whenever I **[do specific things with product]** it works exactly as promised. Not only do I **[specific benefits]** but it makes me feel **[strong emotional reaction]**.

I find I use the product in that way every **[time period: hour / day / week, etc.]**.

It's as if you looked me in the eye and said, '**[Persona's name]**, I promise you **[value promise]**'.

What I didn't expect, and share with other **[why shares with]** by **[mean of 'sharing']** is that you made me feel **[emotion impact]**.

Your product has forever **[how life changed]**.

I first heard of your product while **[activity / place related to title or life role]**. I decided to learn if it was really meant for me, so **[how to get more info]** where you said **[key message promise],** which spoke directly to me. To tell you the truth, at first I was skeptical. But then, when you provided **[activity to induce trust]** I knew you were the right company.

[Influencer] endorsing the product was also key.

Still, I felt **[primary concern / objection]**.

Finally, when **[final action]** I was ready to **[sign up / buy / try]**.

I couldn't wait to get going, so as soon as I could, I **[first product setup / interaction]** to get started, and very quickly tried the **[feature to realize promise]** which made me feel hopeful that I had made the right decision.

Love Letter Example

Dear Tooliers®,

My name is Elisabeth. I must tell you that I love your Marketing Lens™ Diagnosis and Growth Program and I feel compelled to tell you my story.

I am an accounting firm owner who needs more clients. Thing is, I'm not earning enough. But Marketing Lens™ has changed my life.

Whenever I think of investing in marketing activities, I use the Marketing Lens™ and it works exactly as promised. Not only do I discover free ways to attract clients, but it also makes me feel like I really master marketing as a whole. I find myself working on one action to grow my business every other day, for only 15 minutes per day. I started this just one month ago and I already see 10% more enquiries from potential clients.

It's as if you looked me in the eye and said, 'Elisabeth I promise that you will discover ways of getting more customers by yourself without spending a cent.'

What I didn't expect, and I share this with other accounting firm owners in our regular ACCA meetings, is that you made me feel like a great businessperson, not just an accountant. I truly *feel* I own my business now; I am not just a simple accountant who has a job in my own company.

Marketing Lens™ Diagnosis and Growth Program has forever changed how I market our accounting services.

I first heard of your product while browsing The American Institute of CPAs online. I decided to learn if it was really meant for me and I went to www.tooliers.com. You said that I would get answers to questions I had never asked myself and this really resonated with me. To tell you the truth, at first I was skeptical about getting actions tailored to my business and given automatically to me by a computer! No one knows my industry better than me. But then, when you provided the Marketing Lens™ Diagnostic Report I knew you were the right company. Your assessment of why I was not attracting the customers I wanted was spot on. You also showed me what I need to focus on attracting the customers I deserve.

Entrepreneur.com's endorsement of Marketing Lens™ Diagnosis and Growth Program was also key to my decision to check you out. They are a trusted resource with information for every business owner.

Still, even at this stage I felt marketing was too complicated for me. Besides, I truly love performing accounting services, *not* marketing my business. Finally, after having followed the Action Plan on Social Media, I was ready to buy the Marketing Lens™ Growth Program. I understand now that things are not as complicated as they seemed, and that even I can attract and engage online with potential clients for my firm!

I couldn't wait to get going, so as soon as I could, I performed the Marketing Lens™ Diagnosis. I quickly started with the first action on Sales Funnel Tactic, which made me feel comfortable that I'd made the right decision. I see how, by the end of the Growth Program, I will have become a marketing guru for my business; customers will come to us, as bees are attracted to a honeypot. And you know what? I now see myself as *managing an accounting practice*, and no longer as doing accounting services. The latter is the job of my employees!

Love Letter

Want to grow your business and don't know how and where to start?

Or do you have a business challenge you want an expert opinion on?

I love bringing new ideas to the table and contributing to the growth of any kind of business, from e-commerce sites to professional services providers; from retail to entertainment. Every industry has its own particularities, but all have one thing in common: **apply best business practices and your business will succeed.** It's exactly this subject that I've mastered, and I can help any business implement best practices, regardless of size, industry or geography.

So contact me via my website and I'll respond within 24 hours.

www.ozanagiusca.com

If you just want to stay in touch, connect with me on:

- www.facebook.com/giusca.ozana
- plus.google.com/+OzanaGiusca
- www.linkedin.com/in/ozanagiusca
- www.twitter.com/OzanaGiusca
- www.youtube.com/user/ozana197

Glossary of Terms

These definitions are crafted to be as simple as possible, and are explained in the context of this book.

AAA rating - refers to the evaluation of credit worthiness; i.e how trustworthy a company is to do business with. The highest rating is AAA, descending to C (low) and D (even worse).

Action Plan or Fast Track implementation Plan - a step-by-step guide to work on and improve various areas of the business (strategy, sales, marketing, etc.) and sub-areas (educational marketing, writing blogs, building a website, email marketing etc.).

Affiliate Marketing - this is an agreement whereby a business rewards someone (affiliate person or company) for each visitor / customer brought by the affiliate's own marketing efforts, or for each purchase generated by the affiliate, within a time frame.

Attractive Premium - an item included in a pack, together with less interesting items, and sold as a bundle. It's a good way of moving slow-selling products.

Automate / Automating / Automation - using software rather than employees to undertake automatically some processes within the company.

Business-to-business (B2B) - a business that sells to other businesses. Compare with Business-to-Consumer (B2C), which is when the company sells to consumers / individuals.

Better Offer - a product (service) or a bundle of products (services), designed to offer more value (than usual) for the same dollar spent.

Brand - the name, design, symbol, colors or any other feature that identifies one company or product. For example, Coca-Cola is one brand, Fanta is another; they both belong to The Coca-Cola Company.

Branding via Association - linking the brand of one business with a better known brand, so the lesser known brand 'borrows' from the popularity of the other.

Business Doctor - business growth solution consisting of (i) diagnosing a business (see Business Lens®), (ii) designing a customized action plan to optimize and grow the company and (iii) implementing that plan.

Business Lens® - company assessment toolkit to show business owners the naked truth about their company. It identifies unexploited growth potential. It covers everything that matters for the growth of

Glossary of Terms

the business (analyzes in detail 15 business dimensions, including Strategy, Innovation, Leadership, Superstar Organization, Marketing, Sales, Human Resources, Motivation, Support Systems, Follow-Up and Organizational Culture) a Tooliers® service.

Business Lens® Diagnostic - the process of answering multiple choice questions and getting a business evaluation report that shows what the business does well and what it needs to focus on a Tooliers® service.

Buying Criteria - the requirements and rules that one buyer uses to buy a product, such as quality, price, availability, reliability, durability, comfort, habit, safety, freshness, coolness, taste, production methods, etc.

Chunking - grouping together information into ideally sized pieces, so they can be used effectively to produce the outcome one wants without stress or shutdown.

Chunk Down - dealing with smaller parts of information / activities in order to understand or do them effectively. Especially useful when the information / activities are new or complex.

Chunk Up - dealing with larger parts of information / activities in order to understand / accomplish more at once. Especially useful when one faces known information or deals with routine activities

Complementary Product (Service) - product (service) whose use is interrelated with the use of another product (service); e.g. cartridges and printers are complementary products.

Cross Selling - one business selling its product (service) to another business's customers, and vice versa.

Distribution Channel - the path through which products travel from vendors to consumers; e.g. coffee travels from farmer to exporter, to importer, to distributor, and to the retailer who sells to the end user.

Educational Marketing - sharing valuable information with potential customers, for their benefit and to build trust.

Gift with Purchase - providing another product (service) when someone buys a certain product (service); e.g. a sample cream when you buy a perfume.

Host-Parasite Relationship - adding one's product to be sold passively together with another product that is marketed and sold by the other business (the 'parasite' company doesn't do anything to make sales happen). E.g. producer of a dress adds belt from another manufacturer, and promotes and sells the dress with the belt.

Inducement(s) - an incentive to make the offering more appealing to the customer, and the sale sweeter.

Joined Offers - offering one's product together with another product; both parties promote the combined offer.

Joint Venture (JV) - business agreement for a set period, in which each party undertakes some efforts, for the benefit of all parties.

Lead - term used for a potential customer in the first stage of a sales process; i.e. the business made the initial contact with that prospect, be it (directly or indirectly) via the business's website, or via a phone call or meeting.

Lead Nurturing Email - email designed to build relationships and trust with prospective customers in a consistent and relevant manner.

Limited Edition - the manufacturing of a product in a limited quantity, to make it a more interesting purchase for the buyer.

Limited Time Offer - an offer that has a specific deadline, to give potential buyers a clear reason to act without delay.

Limited Stock Offer - a limited number of items made available, to give potential buyers a clear reason to act without delay.

Locking Sales In - securing long-term sales; e.g. signing a long-term contract or ensuring customer comes back for repeat purchase.

Offer Email - an email to promote a product, to ask for a purchase.

Potentials or Prospects - potential customers.

Pre-emptive Anti-competition Strategy - a strategy employed by one business to lead potentials to only consider its offering, thus blocking its competitors even before they are considered by the buyer as potential sellers.

Risk Reversal - marketing strategy based on removing the risks of the buyer to help them make the purchase decision; e.g. 30-day money back guarantee.

ROI (Return on Investment) - a performance measure calculated as the benefit produced by an investment divided by the cost of that investment (expressed as %); commonly used to evaluate the efficiency of an investment or to compare different real or potential investments.

Glossary of Terms

ROTI (Return on Time Invested) - the return on the time invested into an activity or project (valued in dollar amount per hour).

Sales Funnel - a metaphoric description of the sales process from initial contact to final sale. It is called a 'funnel', because there are many leads (cold potentials), and as one gets closer to the sale, the number decreases.

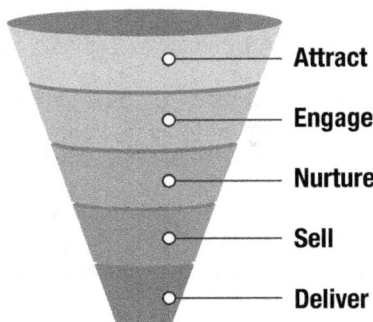

Soft Skills - a cluster of personality traits, social abilities, communication, language, and personal habits that characterize relationships of one person with others.

Tooliers® - online platform with business growth tools designed to help small and mid-sized business owners to take their companies to the next level. Founded by Ozana Gusca.

Ultimate Strategic Position (USP) (not to be confused with Unique Selling Proposition) – the final perception that a company wants to have in the eyes of the customer.

Unique Value Proposition (UVP) - a few words used by one business to tell prospective customers why they should buy their product or use their service; it tells how this business adds more value or better solves a problem than competing businesses (similar to Unique Selling Proposition).

Value Papers - promotional materials (such as flyers, leaflets, brochures, catalogues) that give, besides the usual information / advertising content, monetary value to the holder towards the purchase of the product / service being promoted (such as % discount, $ reduction, gift); the goal is to incentivize a sale.

> 'Any ending is a new beginning.'
> Ozana Giusca

Make the most of the knowledge you have received or gotten from this book and take your business to the next level.

In this series

www.ozanagiusca.com/BusinessUnlimited

www.ingramcontent.com/pod-product-compliance
Lightning Source LLC
Chambersburg PA
CBHW070308230526
45470CB00002B/774